BEAR HUGS

FOR

FROM

Grace and peace to you
from God our Father and from
the Lord Jesus Christ.

Romans 1:7

BEAR HUGS FOR SISTERS

Copyright 2002 by Zondervan
ISBN 0-310-98833-0

Requests for information should be addressed to:

Inspirio, The gift group of Zondervan
Grand Rapids, Michigan 49530
http://www.inspiriogifts.com

Compiler and writer: Lee Stuart
Associate Editor: Molly Detweiler
Project Manager: Patti Matthews
Design: Mark Veldheer
Photography: Photographic Concepts

Printed in China
03 04/HK/4 3

BEAR HUGS

FOR SISTERS

inspirio
The gift group of Zondervan

God for the blessing
of your friendship.

A sister writes her
love on your heart
So wherever you go
you're never apart.

Molly Detweiler

Having you for
a sister always
gives me reason
to celebrate!

Many women do noble things,
but you surpass them all.

Proverbs 31:29

We played hide and seek
for hours each day
We dressed up in Mom's
clothes and put on a play
We made so many memories,
we laughed and we cried
I'll always be thankful that I
had you by my side.

Molly Detweiler

Sisters are the people who give you a tissue, a hug and a shoulder to cry on, even when you're crying so hard that your nose gets runny.

May you be blessed by the LORD,

the Maker of heaven and earth.

Psalm 115:15

Love and faithfulness
meet together;
righteousness and peace
kiss each other.

Psalm 85:10

If we walk in the light,
as God is in the light,
we have fellowship
with one another.

1 John 1:7

For there is no friend like a sister
In calm or stormy weather;
To cheer one on the tedious way,
To fetch one if one goes astray,
To lift one if one totters down,
To strengthen whilst one stands.

Christina Rossetti

Your love has given
me great joy and
encouragement.

Philemon 7

When I'm feeling blue, you always help me see things from a different angle.

I couldn't bear not

having you for a sister.

I'd like to make a wish…
that everyone could have a
sister as wonderful as you!

Talking late at night...
having pillow fights...
These are just a
few of the special
memories that I
cherish about you.

She speaks with wisdom, and faithful instruction is on her tongue.

Proverbs 31:26

The way I see it,
you're *always* a
beautiful person.

Where the Spirit
of the Lord is,
there is freedom.

2 Corinthians 3:17

You are a
woman of noble
character.

Ruth 3:11

Having you for

my sister makes my heart
feel light with joy!

The unfading beauty of a
gentle and quiet spirit...is of
great worth in God's sight.

1 Peter 3:4

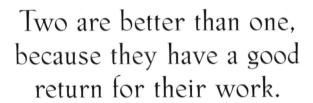

Two are better than one,
because they have a good
return for their work.

Ecclesiastes 4:9

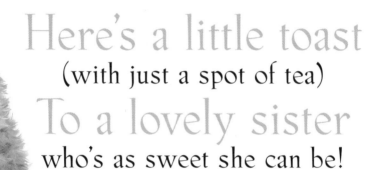

Here's a little toast
(with just a spot of tea)
To a lovely sister
who's as sweet she can be!

There's a special kind of freedom sisters enjoy—freedom to share innermost thoughts, to ask a favor, to show their true feelings; the freedom to simply be themselves.

Anonymous

Like flowers in a garden
we grow in different
directions, and blossom
in our own ways, yet
our roots remain as one.
Each of our lives will
always be a special
part of the other.

Thank you,
my sister, for
allowing me to tell
you anything and
for always keeping
my secrets!

A sister would never
burst your bubble

(except when she has the
chance to see you get gum
all over your face)!

Sisters—

as youngsters they may
share Popsicles, chewing gum,
hair dryers and bedrooms.
When they grow up, they
share confidences, careers
and children, and some even
chat for hours every day.

Roxanne Brown

A woman who fears the LORD
is to be praised.
Give her the reward
she has earned.

Proverbs 31:30–31

Thinking of you...

turns my frown

upside down!

The LORD your God is with you, he is mighty to save. He will take great delight in you, he will quiet you with his love, he will rejoice over you with singing.

Zephaniah 3:17

I've learned so much from you. You taught me everything I needed to know about dressing kittens in doll clothes, making the perfect mud pie and, of course, how to accessorize!

Pat-a-cake,
Pat-a-cake,
Baker's man.
Bake me a cake
as fast as you can.
Roll it, and stamp it,
and mark it with an "S"
and put it in the oven
for my sister and me.
(hopefully it's
chocolate cake!)

With my sister at my side, I feel like I can take on the world!

Barbara

Ruth

Some of my very
best memories
are the times spent with you,
Me   laughing, crying,
and just being
together.

Sometimes when the skies are gray
My sister calls to brighten the day
And after we have said goodbye
The sun comes out to light my sky!

How great is the
love the Father has
lavished on us, that
we should be called
children of God!

1 John 3:1

S is for sensational
I is for interesting
S is for sensitive
T is for tender
E is for encouraging
R is for radiant

When you put them together,
they describe you!

How can we thank God enough
for you in return for all the
joy we have in the presence of
our God because of you?

1 Thessalonians 3:9